3 1526 03246821 4

P9-CCB-210

The Dirt on Pigpen

WITHDRAWN
Harford County Public Library

Charles M. Schulz

Ballantine Books • New York

HARFORD COUNTY
PUBLIC LIBRARY
100 E. Pennsylvania Avenue
Bel Air, MD 21014

A Ballantine Books Trade Paperback Original

Copyright (c) 2007 by United Feature Syndicate, Inc.

All rights reserved.

Published in the United States by Ballantine Books, an imprint of The Random House Publishing Group, a division of Random House, Inc., New York.

BALLANTINE and colophon are registered trademarks of Random House, Inc.

The comic strips in this book were originally published in newspapers worldwide.

ISBN 978-0-345-47984-6

Printed in the United States of America

www.ballantinebooks.com

9 8 7 6 5 4 3 2 1

Book design by Diane Hobbing of Snap-Haus Graphics

The Dirt on

Pigpen

"PEANUTS"
HELLO THERE.. WHAT'S YOUR NAME?
I HAVEN'T GOT A NAME..PEOPLE JUST CALL ME THINGS..REAL INSULTING THINGS...
WHAT DO THEY CALL YOU MOST OF THE TIME?
I'LL TELL YOU IF YOU WON'T LAUGH...
'PIG-PEN'
7-13
SCHULZ

"PEANUTS"
CHARLIE BROWN, HAVE YOU MET LITTLE 'PIG-PEN'?
'PIG-PEN', THIS IS GOOD OL' CHARLIE BROWN..
HI, KID...
ISN'T HE A MESS? LOOK AT HIS HANDS AND FACE...AND THOSE OVERALLS...
7-14
I GOT CLEAN THOUGHTS!
SCHULZ

"PEANUTS"
DON'T YOU WANT TO WASH YOUR HANDS BEFORE YOU EAT, 'PIG-PEN'?
NO, THAT WON'T BE NECESSARY...I'LL JUST POUND THEM TOGETHER..
WHAP! WHAP! WHAP!
!
THAT'S THE WAY THEY CLEAN ERASERS!
7-15
SCHULZ

"PEANUTS" WHAT IN THE WORLD IS **THIS** COMING... A WALKING MUD PUDDLE?

WELL! HELLO THERE, LITTLE DOGGIE!

OH, GOOD GRIEF!

NICE DOGGIE...

OOOO! THOSE DIRTY HANDS!

PAT PAT

SIGH

7-16

SCHULZ

"PEANUTS" HEY, **'PIG-PEN'**! YOUR MOTHER WANTS YOU TO GO HOME, AND TAKE A BATH!

FINE! I'LL GO RIGHT NOW..

??? I SORT OF HAD THE IDEA THAT YOU'D **HATE** BATHS..

OH, NO... I **LIKE** TO TAKE BATHS...

THE WHOLE TROUBLE WITH ME IS THAT I LIKE GETTING DIRTY EVEN BETTER!

7-17

SCHULZ

"PEANUTS" 'PIG-PEN', YOU'RE A MESS!

THANK YOU!

I THINK YOU MUST GO OUT OF YOUR WAY TO GET DIRTY..

NOT AT ALL..

SPLASH SPLASH

!

I JUST DON'T GO OUT OF MY WAY TO STAY CLEAN!

7-20

SCHULZ

"PEANUTS"
HI, PIG-PEN
HI, CHARLIE BROWN...GOT SOME CANDY EH? GONNA GIMME SOME?
LET'S SEE...I'LL FEEL AROUND A BIT UNTIL I FIND A PIECE I LIKE.. OOPS! I SQUASHED ONE.
SOME OF THESE ARE KIND OF STICKY, AREN'T THEY? THAT DOESN'T MATTER, THOUGH...MY HANDS WERE STICKY TO START WITH..
SCHULZ 7-22
WELL, THAT WAS NICE OF HIM...HE WALKED AWAY AND LEFT ME THE WHOLE BAG!
Tm Reg U S Pat Off —All rights reserved Copr 1954 by United Feature Syndicate, Inc

"PEANUTS"
LUCY I'D LIKE TO HAVE YOU MEET 'PIG-PEN'...
BOY!! YOU ARE WELL NAMED, AREN'T YOU? BUT WHO AM I TO BE CRITICAL? WELCOME TO THE GANG
WHACK!
7-23
EVERYBODY STAND STILL UNTIL THE DUST SETTLES!
SCHULZ

"PEANUTS" 'PIG-PEN', YOU'RE A MESS!

WHY DON'T YOU TRY TO BE MORE NEAT?

BEING DIRTY IS MUCH MORE PRACTICAL..

I'M NEVER BOTHERED BY GIRLS OR MOSQUITOES!

7-30   SCHULZ

"PEANUTS" OH, OH! HERE COMES 'PIG-PEN'... AND HE'S CARRYING A BALL..

DON'T TELL ME HE EXPECTS ME TO CATCH A BALL HE'S BEEN HOLDING IN THOSE DIRTY HANDS?!

HERE, DOGGIE..

AAK!

7-31   SCHULZ

"PEANUTS"
'PIG-PEN', YOU'RE AMAZING!
TRUE
IT'S ONLY SEVEN O'CLOCK IN THE MORNING, AND ALREADY YOU'RE A MUDDY MESS!
UH, HUH..
THIS LOOKS LIKE IT'S GOING TO BE A GOOD DAY!
SCHULZ
8-10

"PEANUTS"
HOW ABOUT A PAIL OF SAND, OLD FRIEND?
WELL, ... I GUESS YOU CAN TAKE ONE PAILFUL ...BUT JUST **ONE**... UNDERSTAND?
I UNDERSTAND COMPLETELY.. I GRASP YOUR THOUGHT.. **ONE** PAILFUL... **ONE**..
SCHULZ 8-16
!

"PEANUTS"
'PIG-PEN', YOU'RE A MESS!
YOU'RE A MESS WHEN YOU EAT, A MESS WHEN YOU PLAY AND A MESS WHEN YOU'RE JUST STANDING STILL..
WELL, YOU'LL HAVE TO ADMIT **ONE** THING..
I'M CONSISTENT!
8-18
SCHULZ

"PEANUTS"
HI, 'PIG-PEN'... WHO WON THE GAME?
GAME? WHAT GAME?
OH, I THOUGHT YOU HAD BEEN PLAYING BALL..
YOU LOOK LIKE YOU JUST SLID INTO SECOND BASE
INSULTS.. THAT'S ALL I HEAR! **INSULTS!**
8-23
SCHULZ

"PEANUTS"
HERE COMES THE COWBOY SHOW, 'PIG-PEN'!
HOORAY!
Clap! Clap! Clap! Clap!
NOW, LOOK HERE...EITHER WASH THOSE HANDS OR **STOP APPLAUDING!**
8-30
SCHULZ

"PEANUTS"
I'M GOING TO FIND 'PIG-PEN', AND PERSONALLY GIVE HIM A GOOD SCRUBBING!
!?!
YOU'RE ALREADY CLEAN! WHAT A SURPRISE!!!
I GUESS THERE'S SOME HOPE FOR HIM, AFTER ALL..
SCHULZ 9-6

"PEANUTS"
WHY DO YOU HAVE TO BE SO SLOPPY, 'PIG-PEN'?!
DON'T YOU KNOW THAT PEOPLE WILL NEVER ADMIRE YOU?
THEY WON'T?
OF COURSE NOT! NO ONE LIKES TO BE... TO BE... TO BE....
SCHULZ 9-8

"PEANUTS"
WELL, SCHROEDER! I'M SURPRISED AT YOU!
YOU USED TO BE SO NEAT! AND NOW YOU'VE LET THIS LITTLE 'PIG-PEN' INFLUENCE YOU!
WELL, YOU TWO BETTER STICK TOGETHER BECAUSE NOBODY ELSE WILL WANT TO GO NEAR YOU!
!
SCHULZ 9-9

"PEANUTS"
IT'S AWFUL, CHARLIE BROWN! FIRST IT WAS SCHROEDER, AND NOW IT'S SNOOPY!
THEY'RE A MESS! DIRTY HANDS..DIRTY FACES..DIRTY CLOTHES!
THEY'VE LET 'PIG-PEN' INFLUENCE THEM, AND I THINK THAT'S AWFUL!
9-10
WHAT'S SO AWFUL ABOUT IT?
SCHULZ

"PEANUTS"
WE DECIDED YOU WERE RIGHT, PATTY...
SCHROEDER, SNOOPY AND I AREN'T LETTING OURSELVES BE INFLUENCED BY 'PIG-PEN' ANY MORE..
YOU SHOULD SEE US...WE'RE SO CLEAN! YOU'D REALLY BE PROUD OF US..
Tm. Reg. U. S. Pat. Off.—All rights reserved
Copr. 1954 by United Feature Syndicate, Inc.
I WOULD?
SCHULZ
9-11

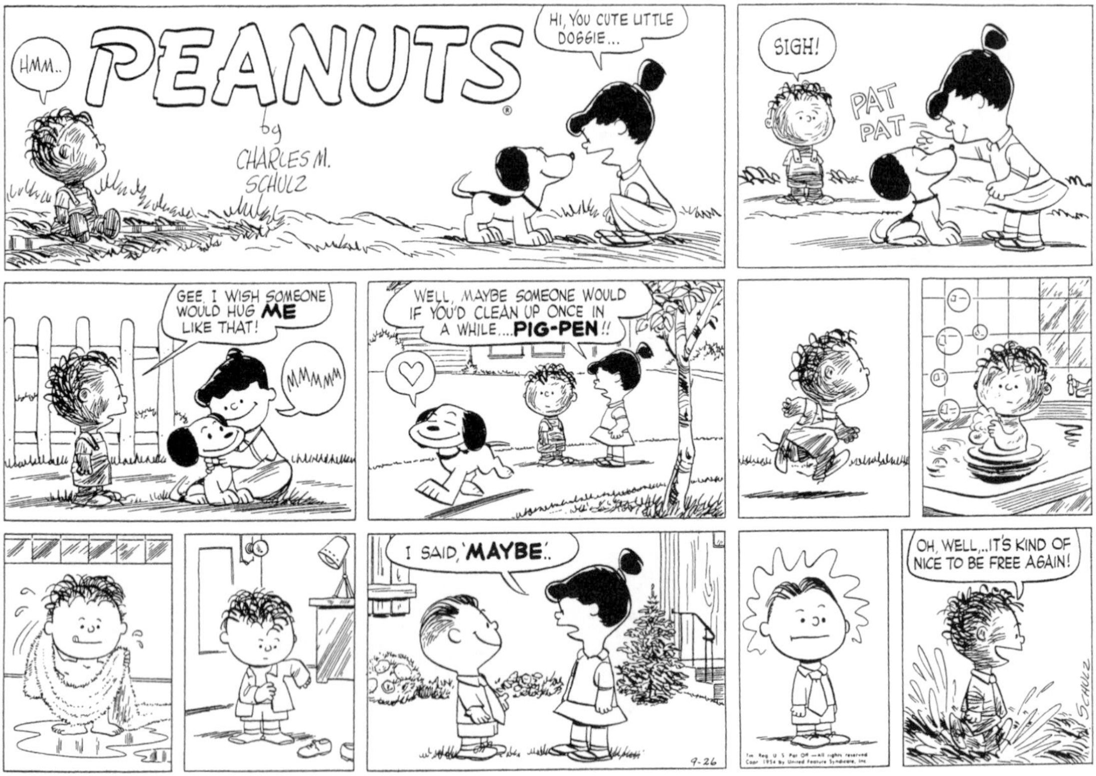
HMM..
PEANUTS
by CHARLES M. SCHULZ
HI, YOU CUTE LITTLE DOGGIE...
SIGH!
PAT PAT
GEE, I WISH SOMEONE WOULD HUG **ME** LIKE THAT!
MMMMM
WELL, MAYBE SOMEONE WOULD IF YOU'D CLEAN UP ONCE IN A WHILE....**PIG-PEN**!!
I SAID, '**MAYBE**'.
9-26
Tm Reg U S Pat Off —All rights reserved
Copr 1954 by United Feature Syndicate, Inc
OH, WELL,..IT'S KIND OF NICE TO BE FREE AGAIN!
SCHULZ

"PEANUTS" O.K., GIMME THE TOWEL..

IS THAT THE BEST YOU CAN DO, 'PIG-PEN'?

YOU JUST BARELY TOUCHED YOUR FACE!

I KNOW IT.. THAT'S ALL THAT'S NECESSARY..

I WASH JUST ENOUGH SO THAT I CAN SEE WHERE I'M GOING!

10-22 SCHULZ

"PEANUTS" 'PIG-PEN' YOU'RE A DISGRACE TO THE NEIGHBORHOOD

WHY, THE WAY YOU LOOK AND ACT, YOU'RE NO BETTER THAN AN ANIMAL!

WHAT DID I SAY?!

WAIT, SNOOPY, WAIT! I DIDN'T MEAN IT THAT WAY... I'M SORRY... I'M...

SCHULZ 11-4

"PEANUTS" 'PIG-PEN' I'D LIKE TO SEE JUST WHAT YOU LOOK LIKE ONCE WHEN YOU'RE NOT DIRTY..

WELL! HE TOOK THE HINT.. THAT WAS A SURPRISE!

HERE'S A SNAPSHOT TAKEN OF ME ONE DAY LAST JULY WHEN I WAS ALL CLEANED UP..

11-6 SCHULZ

17

HEY! WAIT UP!
PEANUTS
by CHARLES M. SCHULZ
POOR OL' 'PIG-PEN'... I'LL BET HE COULD RAISE A CLOUD OF DUST RUNNING ON A SIDEWALK!
HERE, CHARLIE BROWN... I'VE GOT A PIECE OF CANDY FOR YOU..
GEE...I CAN'T GET IT OUT OF MY POCKET.. IT'S STUCK...
THERE!
OH, GOOD GRIEF!
I'LL BRUSH THE LINT OFF FOR YOU,.. AND SCRAPE THIS OLD GUM OFF THE BEST I CAN...
I FEEL SICK
WELL, WHY DON'T YOU EAT IT?
I WILL, 'PIG-PEN', I WILL...I JUST...I.. I..
WHOOPS! I DROPPED IT!
!
GULP!
ZOOM
Tm. Reg. U. S. Pat Off.—All rights reserved
Copr. 1954 by United Feature Syndicate, Inc.
PSST... SNOOPY, OL' PAL...YOU'D BETTER COME HOME WITH ME, AND HAVE A DRINK OF WATER..
?
SCHULZ
12-5

"PEANUTS"
C'MON, AND SEE THE SNOWMAN 'PIG-PEN' MADE
SAY, I'LL BET PLAYING AROUND IN THE SNOW KEPT HIM CLEAN, DIDN'T IT?
ON THE CONTRARY...
THE WORLD'S DIRTIEST SNOWMAN!
SCHULZ

"PEANUTS"
'PIG-PEN', HAVE YOU EVER HEARD THAT OLD SAYING?
WHAT OLD SAYING?
'CLEANLINESS IS NEXT TO GODLINESS'
OH, YES... MANY TIMES..
THEN WHY DON'T YOU FOLLOW IT?
BECAUSE WITH ME, CHARLIE BROWN, CLEANLINESS IS NEXT TO IMPOSSIBLE!
SCHULZ

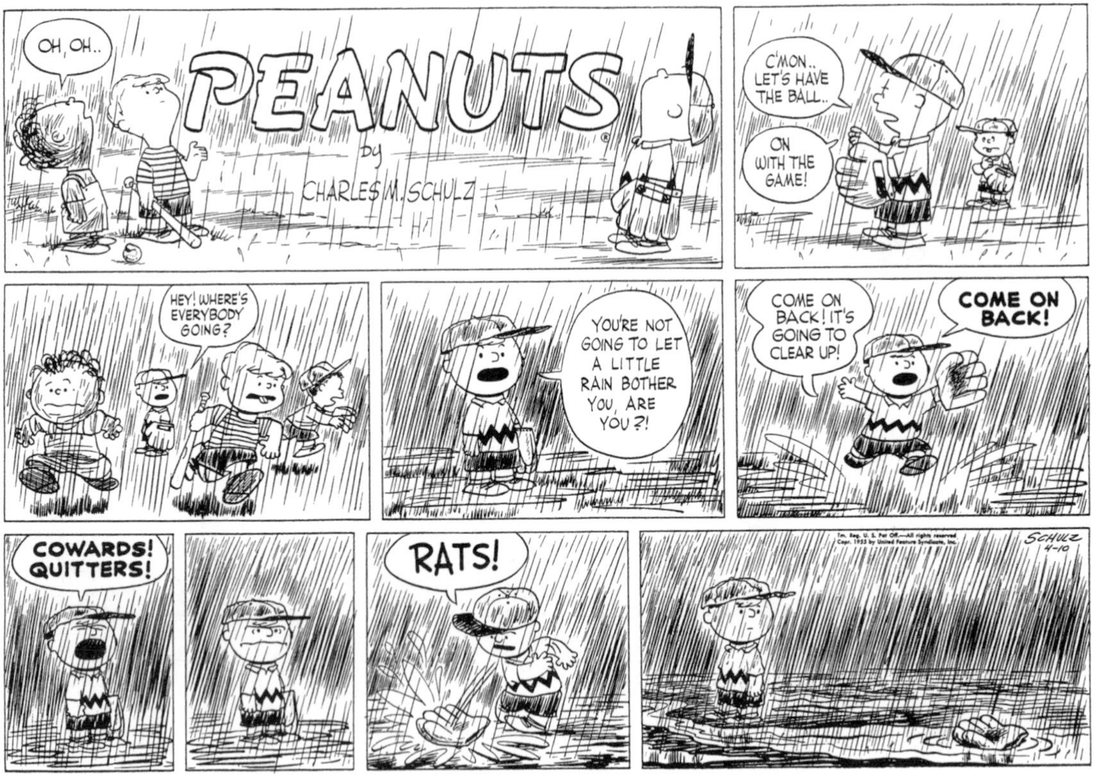
OH, OH..
PEANUTS
by
CHARLES M. SCHULZ
C'MON.. LET'S HAVE THE BALL..
ON WITH THE GAME!
HEY! WHERE'S EVERYBODY GOING?
YOU'RE NOT GOING TO LET A LITTLE RAIN BOTHER YOU, ARE YOU?!
COME ON BACK! IT'S GOING TO CLEAR UP!
COME ON BACK!
COWARDS! QUITTERS!
RATS!
Tm. Reg. U. S. Pat Off.—All rights reserved
Copr. 1955 by United Feature Syndicate, Inc.
SCHULZ 4-10

"PEANUTS"
HI, 'PIG-PEN'.. WHERE YA GOIN'?
AS THE DUCK IS DRAWN TO THE POND, AND AS THE RABBIT IS DRAWN TO THE BRIER PATCH..
SO AM I DRAWN TO THE MUD PUDDLE!
Good grief!
SCHULZ
4-18

"PEANUTS"
'PIG-PEN,' WHY ARE YOU SO MESSY?
DO YOU SUPPOSE IT'S HEREDITARY, OR IS IT YOUR ENVIRONMENT?
IT MUST BE MY ENVIRONMENT...
I'M COVERED WITH IT!
4-27
SCHULZ

"PEANUTS"
JUST LOOK AT THAT 'PIG-PEN'..
?
ISN'T HE AWFUL?
TERRIBLE .. JUST TERRIBLE!
A REAL 'GOOD-FOR-NOTHING'..
I'LL SAY... A COMPLETE FLOP!
I'M WELL-READ!
4-28
SCHULZ

"PEANUTS"
SLIDE, CHARLIE BROWN!! SLIDE!
NO! NO! DON'T!!
NO MORE SLIDING INTO HOME!!
?
YOU'RE WEARING DOWN THE EARTH!
SCHULZ
5-4

"PEANUTS"
HA HA HA HA HA..
GO AHEAD AND LAUGH, CHARLIE BROWN! SOMEDAY I'LL SHOW YOU!!
?
IT'S NOT NICE TO LAUGH AT A PERSON'S AMBITIONS!!! BUT, BY GOLLY, I'LL SHOW HIM!
SOMEDAY I'LL BE A 'WHITE-COLLAR WORKER'!
6-17
SCHULZ

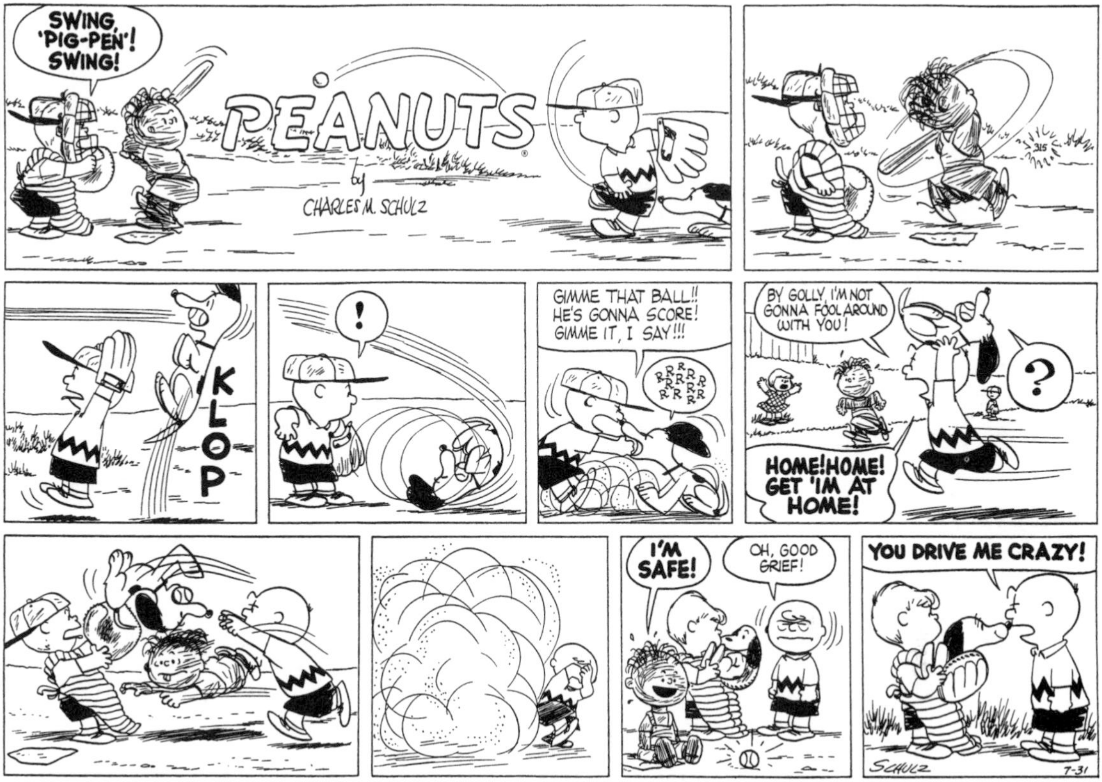
SWING, 'PIG-PEN'! SWING!
PEANUTS
by CHARLES M. SCHULZ
KLOP
!
GIMME THAT BALL!! HE'S GONNA SCORE! GIMME IT, I SAY!!!
RRRRRRRRRR
BY GOLLY, I'M NOT GONNA FOOL AROUND WITH YOU!
?
HOME! HOME! GET 'IM AT HOME!
I'M SAFE!
OH, GOOD GRIEF!
YOU DRIVE ME CRAZY!
SCHULZ
7-31

"PEANUTS"
RING
TRICKS OR TREATS!
WHAT?!
I'VE BEEN AWAY..
11-14
SCHULZ

"PEANUTS"
I'VE DECIDED THAT CLEAN HANDS ARE VERY IMPORTANT...
WELL, GOOD FOR YOU, "PIG-PEN"...
WHAT MADE YOU DECIDE THAT?
I DISCOVERED THAT ALL THAT DIRT WAS CLOGGING UP MY FINGERPRINTS!
SCHULZ
11-15

"PEANUTS"
?
!
11-16
"PIG-PEN," YOU'RE THE ONLY PERSON I KNOW WHO CAN GET DIRTY JUST WALKING ALONG THE STREET!
SCHULZ

"PEANUTS"
'PIG-PEN,' YOU'RE AN ABSOLUTE MESS!
HERE, I WANT YOU TO LOOK AT YOURSELF IN THIS MIRROR...
NOW! AREN'T YOU ASHAMED?
ON THE CONTRARY...
I DIDN'T THINK I LOOKED THAT GOOD!
1-7
SCHULZ

"PEANUTS"
'PIG-PEN,' IT'S BAD ENOUGH THAT YOU'RE AS DIRTY AS YOU ARE..
BUT COULDN'T YOU AT LEAST TIE YOUR SHOELACES?
?
WHAT DO YOU WANT ME TO BE....
INCONSISTENT?
1-25
SCHULZ

"PEANUTS"
JUST HOW WOULD YOU DESCRIBE 'PIG-PEN' VIOLET?
!
DIRTY HANDS, DIRTY FACE, DIRTY SHIRT AND DIRTY OVERALLS..
A PERFECT DESCRIPTION!
SHE FORGOT ONE THING...
1-28
AN IMMACULATELY CLEAN CONSCIENCE!
SCHULZ

"PEANUTS"
ISN'T THAT 'PIG-PEN' A MESS?
LOOK AT HIS CLOTHES..AND HIS HAIR...AND THAT DIRTY FACE..
YOU KNOW WHAT HE LOOKS LIKE?
WHAT?
4-26
A HUMAN SOIL-BANK!
SCHULZ

PEANUTS
WELL, I'LL BE!
I'VE BEEN AFRAID THIS WOULD HAPPEN SOME DAY... MOM!
I'VE SCRUBBED, AN' SCRUBBED, AN' SCRUBBED, BUT I CAN'T GET CLEAN..
I THINK I'VE REACHED THE 'POINT OF NO RETURN'!
6-19
SCHULZ

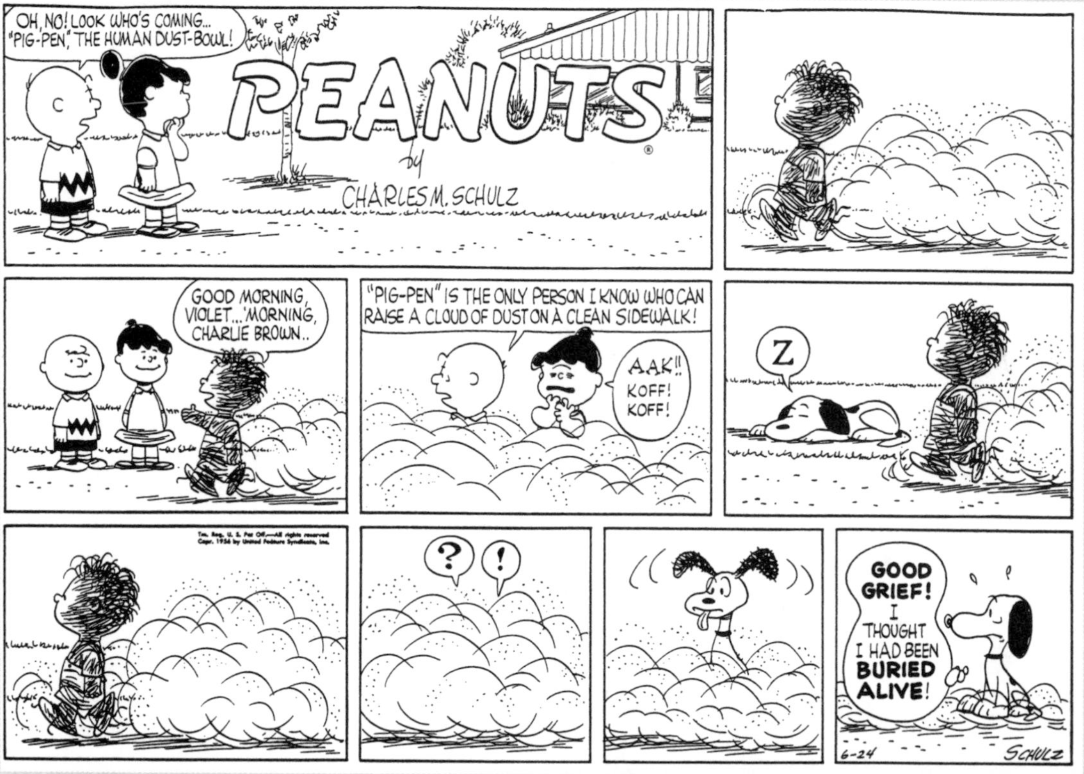
OH, NO! LOOK WHO'S COMING... "PIG-PEN," THE HUMAN DUST-BOWL!
PEANUTS
by CHARLES M. SCHULZ
GOOD MORNING, VIOLET... 'MORNING, CHARLIE BROWN..
"PIG-PEN" IS THE ONLY PERSON I KNOW WHO CAN RAISE A CLOUD OF DUST ON A CLEAN SIDEWALK!
AAK!! KOFF! KOFF!
Z
?
!
GOOD GRIEF! I THOUGHT I HAD BEEN BURIED ALIVE!
6-24
SCHULZ

PEANUTS
BOY, IT'S HOT TODAY...
GOOD MORNING, PATTY... GOOD MORNING, CHARLIE BROWN... BEAUTIFUL DAY, ISN'T IT?
THE HEAT DOESN'T SEEM TO BE BOTHERING 'PIG-PEN' MUCH..
I THINK HE'S PROBABLY COOLED BY SEVERAL LAYERS OF CLAY!
7-31
SCHULZ

PEANUTS
!
RATS!
8-13
IN ONE MINUTE THE RAIN HAS WASHED AWAY WHAT TOOK ME ALL DAY TO ACCOMPLISH!
SCHULZ

PEANUTS
"PIG-PEN," WHY ARE YOU ALWAYS SO DIRTY?
WHEN IN THE WORLD ARE YOU GOING TO CLEAN UP?
I HAVE AFFIXED TO ME THE DIRT AND DUST OF COUNTLESS AGES..
WHO AM I TO DISTURB HISTORY?
SCHULZ
9-17

PEANUTS

"PIG-PEN" IS THE ONLY PERSON I KNOW WHO CAN GET DIRTY WALKING IN A SNOWSTORM!

2-25

PEANUTS

I THINK EVERYONE ADMIRES YOUR INDEPENDENT SPIRIT, "PIG-PEN."

YOU HAVE REMAINED DIRTY WHEN EVERYONE ELSE WAS CLEAN!

OH, I'VE BEEN INDEPENDENT ALL RIGHT..

BUT LATELY, IT'S BEEN DIFFICULT.. TIMES CHANGE...WE ALL GROW A LITTLE OLDER EACH DAY....

I'LL TELL YOU FRANKLY, CHARLIE BROWN... I'M SCARED!

2-26

PEANUTS

HEY, AREN'T WE SHORT ONE MAN? WHERE'S 'PIG-PEN'?

HE'S RIGHT WHERE YOU PUT HIM...AT SECOND BASE..

OH, YES, SO HE IS..

HE'S HARD TO SEE BECAUSE HE BLENDS IN WITH THE DIRT ON THE INFIELD!

4-18

PEANUTS
HI, "PIG-PEN".. WHAT ARE YOU DOING?
NOTHING... I JUST LIKE TO SIT HERE AND WATCH THE REST OF THE WORLD GO BY
Tm. Reg. U. S. Pat Off.—All rights reserved Copr. 1957 by United Feature Syndicate, Inc.
UH HUH ..
IT LOOKS LIKE A LOT OF IT HAS STAYED WITH YOU!
SCHULZ
5-24

PEANUTS
CHOMP CHOMP CHOMP
?
CHOMP CHOMP CHOMP
GULP
Tm. Reg. U. S. Pat Off.—All rights reserved Copr. 1957 by United Feature Syndicate, Inc.
WELL THAT'S THE LAST OF THE EASTER EGGS!
5-25
SCHULZ

PEANUTS
"PIG-PEN" NEVER SAYS VERY MUCH, DOES HE?
HE'S AFRAID TO... WHENEVER HE TALKS, THE DIRT ON HIS FACE FLAKES OFF, AND FALLS ON THE GROUND BY HIS FEET..
THAT'S NOT TRUE!!
Tm. Reg. U. S. Pat Off.—All rights reserved
Copr. 1957 by United Feature Syndicate, Inc.
5-30
SCHULZ

PEANUTS
HI, CHARLIE BROWN..
HI, "PIG-PEN"
Tm. Reg. U. S. Pat Off.—All rights reserved
Copr. 1957 by United Feature Syndicate, Inc.
5-31
THAT'S THE ONLY KID I KNOW WHO CAN RAISE A CLOUD OF DUST WALKING IN THE RAIN!
SCHULZ

PEANUTS

I'M GOING DOWN TO THE PARK, AND I'M GOING TO WALK CLEAR AROUND IT..

WELL, HAVE A GOOD TIME..

THANK YOU...

6-1

Tm. Reg. U. S. Pat. Off.—All rights reserved
Copr. 1967 by United Feature Syndicate, Inc.

ONE THING ABOUT "PIG-PEN"... HE'LL NEVER HAVE ANY TROUBLE FINDING HIS WAY HOME!

SCHULZ

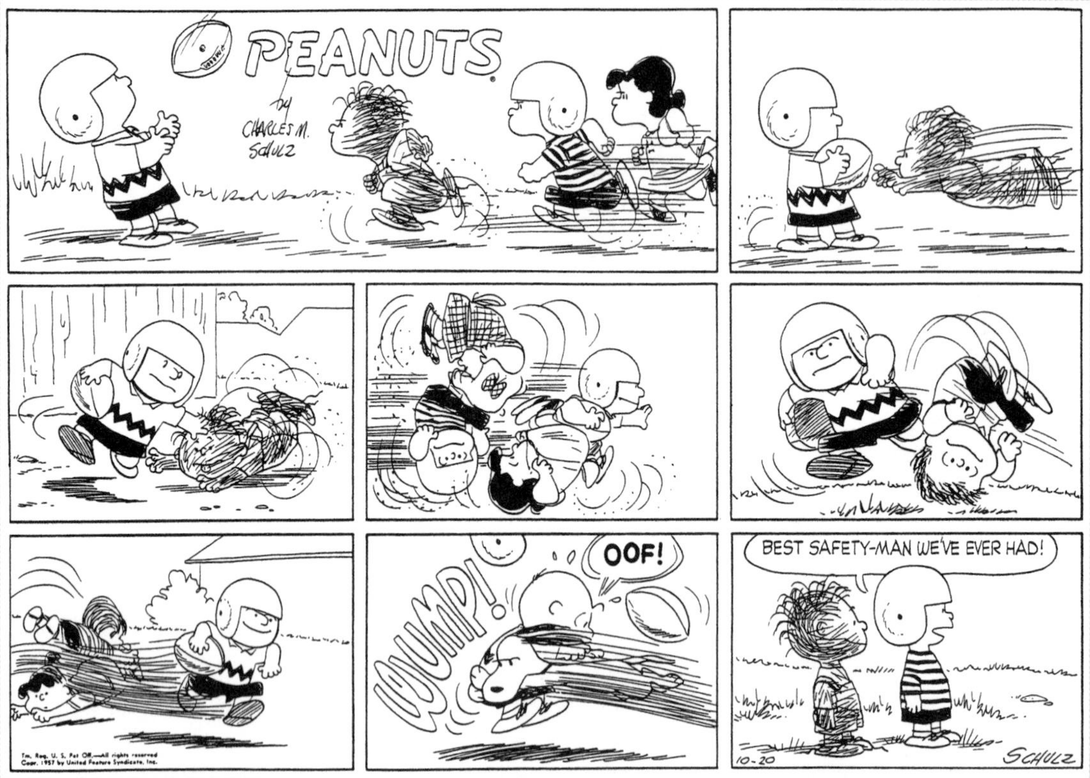
PEANUTS
by CHARLES M. SCHULZ
WUMP!
OOF!
BEST SAFETY-MAN WE'VE EVER HAD!
10-20
SCHULZ
Tm. Reg. U. S. Pat Off.—All rights reserved
Copr. 1957 by United Feature Syndicate, Inc.

NOW'S THE TIME FOR A GOOD PASS PLAY!
PEANUTS
by CHARLES M. SCHULZ
ALL RIGHT, MEN, LET'S GET IN THERE THIS TIME, AND SMEAR 'EM!
NOW, LISTEN CAREFULLY
SCHROEDER HIKES THE BALL TO YOU, LINUS, AND YOU FADE BACK, AND THROW ME A LONG PASS..
NOW, ARE YOU SURE YOU UNDERSTAND?
OF COURSE, I UNDERSTAND!
WELL, I HOPE SO..
SIGNALS! THIRTY-THREE! EIGHTEEN! FORTY-NINE!
HIKE!
PASS IT!
Tm. Reg. U. S. Pat. Off.—All rights reserved
Copr. 1957 by United Feature Syndicate, Inc.
10-27
SCHULZ

PEANUTS
'PIG-PEN,' JUST LOOK AT YOU! YOU'RE A DISGRACE! WHY, YOU'RE A..
STOP RIGHT THERE! BE CAREFUL WHAT YOU SAY!
Tm. Reg. U. S. Pat. Off.—All rights reserved Copr. 1957 by United Feature Syndicate, Inc.
REMEMBER, THIS SOIL AND I ARE AS ONE..
WHEN YOU CRITICIZE ME, YOU CRITICIZE THE SOIL ON WHICH YOU STAND!
11-16
SCHULZ

PEANUTS
Christmas Greetings FROM SHERMY...
LUCY
PIG-PEN
VIOLET
PATTY
Tm. Reg. U. S. Pat. Off.—All rights reserved Copr. 1957 by United Feature Syndicate, Inc
SNOOPY
SCHROEDER
12-25
LINUS
AND GOOD OL' CHARLIE BROWN
SCHULZ

PEANUTS
by CHARLES M. SCHULZ
HI, CHARLIE BROWN... HOW'S THE FRIEND OF ALL MANKIND?
HA HAHA
GOOD GRIEF!
HA HA HA HA!
WELL, IF IT ISN'T CHARLIE BROWN!
GOOD OL' WISHY-WASHY CHARLIE BROWN!
HA HA HA HA HA!
HI, CHARLIE BROWN... IS THAT YOUR HEAD, OR ARE YOU HIDING BEHIND A BALLOON?
HAHAHAHAHAHA
CLICK!
Tm. Reg. U. S. Pat Off.—All rights reserved
Copr. 1958 by United Feature Syndicate, Inc.
"...AND WHAT, IN ALL THIS WORLD, IS MORE DELIGHTFUL THAN THE GAY WONDERFUL LAUGHTER OF LITTLE CHILDREN?"
2-23
SCHULZ

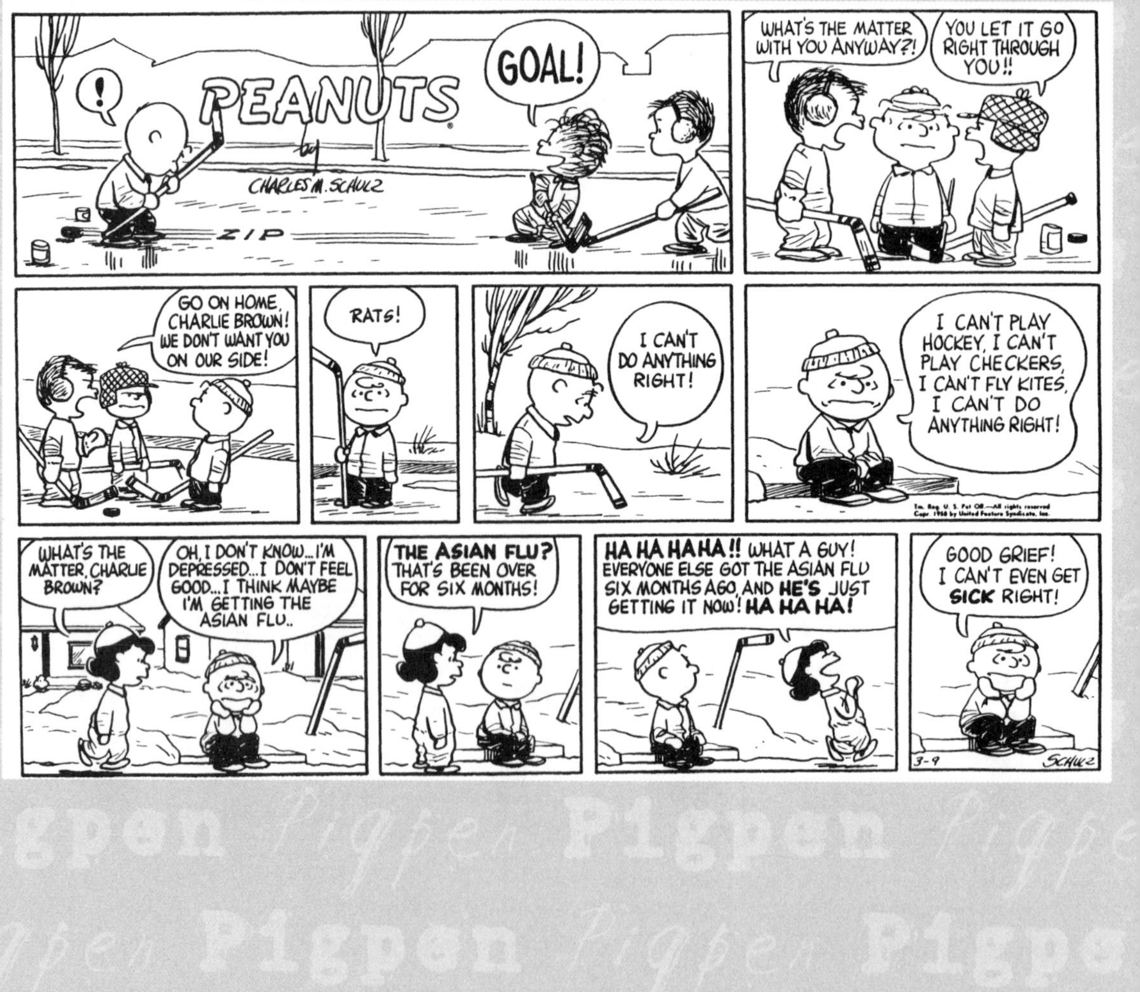
!
PEANUTS
by CHARLES M. SCHULZ
GOAL!
ZIP
WHAT'S THE MATTER WITH YOU ANYWAY?!
YOU LET IT GO RIGHT THROUGH YOU!!
GO ON HOME, CHARLIE BROWN! WE DON'T WANT YOU ON OUR SIDE!
RATS!
I CAN'T DO ANYTHING RIGHT!
I CAN'T PLAY HOCKEY, I CAN'T PLAY CHECKERS, I CAN'T FLY KITES, I CAN'T DO ANYTHING RIGHT!
Tm. Reg. U. S. Pat Off.—All rights reserved
Copr. 1958 by United Feature Syndicate, Inc.
WHAT'S THE MATTER, CHARLIE BROWN?
OH, I DON'T KNOW...I'M DEPRESSED...I DON'T FEEL GOOD...I THINK MAYBE I'M GETTING THE ASIAN FLU..
THE ASIAN FLU? THAT'S BEEN OVER FOR SIX MONTHS!
HA HA HA HA!! WHAT A GUY! EVERYONE ELSE GOT THE ASIAN FLU SIX MONTHS AGO, AND HE'S JUST GETTING IT NOW! HA HA HA!
GOOD GRIEF! I CAN'T EVEN GET SICK RIGHT!
3-9
SCHULZ

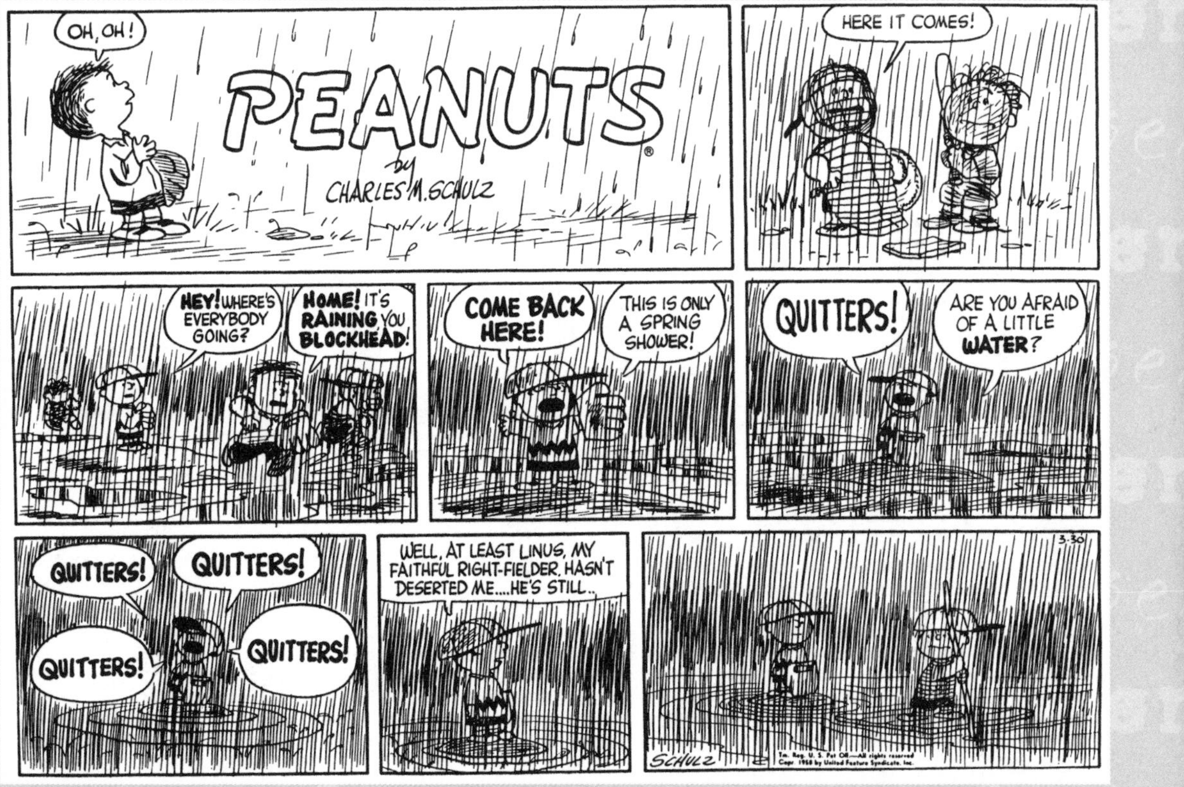
OH, OH!
PEANUTS
by CHARLES M. SCHULZ
HERE IT COMES!
HEY! WHERE'S EVERYBODY GOING?
HOME! IT'S RAINING YOU BLOCKHEAD!
COME BACK HERE!
THIS IS ONLY A SPRING SHOWER!
QUITTERS!
ARE YOU AFRAID OF A LITTLE WATER?
QUITTERS!
QUITTERS!
QUITTERS!
QUITTERS!
WELL, AT LEAST LINUS, MY FAITHFUL RIGHT-FIELDER, HASN'T DESERTED ME....HE'S STILL..
3-30
SCHULZ
Tm. Reg. U. S. Pat. Off.—All rights reserved
Copr. 1958 by United Feature Syndicate, Inc.

PEANUTS
HI, "PIG-PEN"!
HI, CHARLIE BROWN..WOULD YOU LIKE A JELLY BEAN?
WELL, I...UH...I DON'T KNOW.. I... I MEAN...I...UH...UH..
Tm. Reg. U. S. Pat Off.—All rights reserved
Copr. 1958 by United Feature Syndicate, Inc.
OH, DON'T WORRY..THEY'RE CLEAN.. THEY HAVEN'T BEEN ON THE GROUND OR ANYTHING..
IN FACT, I'VE BEEN HOLDING THEM IN MY HANDS EVER SINCE EASTER!
6-21
SCHULZ

PEANUTS ARE YOU THROW-ING AWAY THOSE GOOD JELLY BEANS, "PIG-PEN"?

I HAD TO..

TM Reg. U.S. Pat. Off.—all rights reserved
Copr. 1964 by United Feature Syndicate, Inc.

I'VE BEEN CARRYING THEM AROUND IN MY HANDS FOR ABOUT SIX WEEKS..

I THINK THEY WERE BEGINNING TO FERMENT!

5-22   SCHULZ

PEANUTS
by
CHARLES M. SCHULZ
YOU'RE SLOWING DOWN, "PIG-PEN"...
WAIT A MINUTE...I THINK THERE'S SOME SAND IN MY SHOES...
Tm. Reg. U. S. Pat. Off.—All rights reserved
THERE...THAT'S BETTER!
I JUST CAN'T RUN IF I HAVE SOMETHING IN MY SHOE...
8-10
good grief!
SCHULZ

PEANUTS
"WE ARE HERE TO TELL YOU OF A WONDROUS LIGHT"
I'M SUNK!
"A WONDROUS LIGHT THAT WAS A STAR"
I WONDER IF THERE'S ANY WAY I COULD GET OUT OF HERE...
"THE WISE MEN SAW THE STAR, AND FOLLOWED IT FROM AFAR.."
PSST... LUCY..
"THEY FOUND THE STABLE IN THE NIGHT BENEATH THE STAR SO BIG AND BRIGHT.."
WHAT'S THE MATTER?
I CAN'T REMEMBER MY PIECE!
"THE WISE-MEN LEFT THE PRESENTS THERE...GIFTS SO PRECIOUS AND SO RARE.."
WADDYA MEAN, YOU CAN'T REMEMBER IT?
I CAN'T REMEMBER IT!
"LOOK UP, LOOK UP, THE STAR STILL STANDS, SEEN BY MILLIONS IN MANY LANDS.."
YOU BETTER REMEMBER IT RIGHT NOW, YOU BLOCKHEAD, OR WHEN WE GET HOME, I'LL SLUG YOU A GOOD ONE!
"THE STAR THAT SHONE AT BETHLEHEM STILL SHINES FOR US TODAY!"
12-21
Tm. Reg. U. S. Pat. Off.—All rights reserved
Copr. 1958 by United Feature Syndicate, Inc.
MERRY CHRISTMAS
THANK YOU..
SCHULZ

PEANUTS I JUST DON'T UNDERSTAND..

"PIG-PEN," HOW IN THE WORLD DO YOU MANAGE TO GET SO DIRTY?!

WELL, IT'S KIND OF HARD TO SAY..

I GUESS THERE ARE SOME THINGS WE WILL NEVER KNOW IN THIS LIFETIME!

5-16 SCHULZ

PEANUTS HEY, C'MON!

CHARLIE BROWN HAD A BABY SISTER! HE'S HANDING OUT CHOCOLATE CIGARS!

CONGRATULATIONS, CHARLIE BROWN!

THANK YOU, 'PIG-PEN'..

NOT BAD..THIS SHOULD HAPPEN MORE OFTEN!

5-30

SCHULZ

PEANUTS
I THINK IT'S TIME TO GO HOME AND TAKE A SHOWER..
11-23
GOING TO GET ALL CLEANED UP, EH, "PIG-PEN"?
Tm. Reg. U. S. Pat. Off.—All rights reserved
Copr. 1959 by United Feature Syndicate, Inc.
WELL, I'VE LEARNED NEVER TO EXPECT TOO MUCH FROM A SHOWER...
I HAVE TO BE SATISFIED IF IT JUST SETTLES THE DUST!
SCHULZ

PEANUTS
HI, "PIG-PEN"... YOU LOOK PRETTY CLEAN TODAY FOR A CHANGE
WELL, IT'S A PROBLEM, CHARLIE BROWN..
I'M CLEAN NOW, BUT I DON'T KNOW HOW LONG IT WILL LAST..
11-24
!
YOU CAN SEE WHAT I'M UP AGAINST!
SCHULZ

PEANUTS
IT'S FANTASTIC!
I'M PERFECTLY CLEAN NOW, BUT JUST LET ME STEP OUT OF THE HOUSE FOR ONE MINUTE...
WHAM!
YOU KNOW WHAT I AM? I'M A DUST MAGNET!
11-25
SCHULZ

PEANUTS — DID IT EVER OCCUR TO YOU THAT "PIG-PEN" MIGHT BE CARRYING THE DIRT AND DUST OF SOME PAST CIVILIZATION?

11-26

NOTICE HOW THE DUST CLINGS TO HIM...

HE COULD HAVE ON HIM SOME OF THE SOIL OF ANCIENT BABYLON

SORT OF MAKES YOU WANT TO TREAT ME WITH MORE RESPECT, DOESN'T IT?

Reg. U.S. Pat. Off.—all rights reserved
Copr. 1959 by United Feature Syndicate, Inc.

PEANUTS
JUST THINK OF IT..THE DIRT AND DUST OF FAR-OFF LANDS BLOWING OVER HERE AND SETTLING ON "PIG-PEN"!
IT STAGGERS THE IMAGINATION! HE MAY BE CARRYING SOIL THAT WAS TROD UPON BY SOLOMON OR NEBUCHADNEZZAR OR GENGHIS KHAN!
!
THAT'S TRUE, ISN'T IT?
Tm. Reg. U. S. Pat. Off.—All rights reserved Copr. 1959 by United Feature Syndicate, Inc.
11-27
SUDDENLY I FEEL LIKE ROYALTY!
SCHULZ

PEANUTS
POOR OL' "PIG-PEN"
THEY SAY HE CARRIES ON HIM THE DIRT AND DUST OF ANCIENT CIVILIZATIONS...
Tm. Reg. U. S. Pat. Off.—All rights reserved Copr. 1959 by United Feature Syndicate, Inc.
11-28
HISTORY IS PASSING BEFORE MY EYES!
SCHULZ

PEANUTS

I OWE YOU AN APOLOGY, "PIG-PEN". I'VE BEEN TEASING YOU A LOT LATELY..

BUT WHO AM **I** TO TEASE **YOU**? YOU MAY BE DIRTY, BUT AT LEAST YOU HAVE CHARACTER!

ME? I'M **BLAH**! THAT'S JUST WHAT I AM..**BLAH**! I'M COMPLETELY **BLAH**! I WAS BORN **BLAH**, AND I'LL DIE **BLAH**!

WHEN YOU'RE LOOKING AT **ME** YOU'RE LOOKING AT THE ALL-TIME NUMBER-ONE CHAMPION **BLAH**!!

PEANUTS
by SCHULZ
I CAN'T STAND IT!
LOOK AT 'EM ALL LAUGHING AND ENJOYING THEMSELVES WITH THEIR VALENTINES!
I SENT EVERYONE I KNOW A VALENTINE, BUT DID I GET ANY IN RETURN? NO! NOT A SINGLE ONE!
EVERYBODY GETS VALENTINES EXCEPT ME! NOBODY LIKES ME!
LOOK AT 'EM! THEY ALL GOT VALENTINES! EVERYBODY GOT VALENTINES EXCEPT ME!
EVEN "PIG-PEN" GETS VALENTINES...
BUT DO I? NO!
I GET AS MANY VALENTINES AS A DOG!!
!
SIGH
2-14
SCHULZ

PEANUTS by SCHULZ

HI, SNOOPY...HI SHERMY...GLAD YOU MADE IT.. HI, PIG-PEN...

HI, VIOLET...HOW'S THE WORLD'S PRETTIEST THIRD BASEMAN? HI, LINUS...HI, LUCY...

HI, PATTY...HI, SCHROEDER...HOW'S THE OL' THROWIN' ARM?

WELL, IT'S REAL GOOD SEEING YOU ALL HERE READY TO BEGIN THE NEW BASEBALL SEASON...

DUE TO THE RAIN TODAY, WE WILL FOLLOW THE INCLEMENT WEATHER SCHEDULE...THIS MEANS STUDYING OUR SIGNALS..

NOW A GOOD BASEBALL TEAM FUNCTIONS ON THE KNOWLEDGE OF ITS SIGNALS.. THIS YEAR WE WILL TRY TO KEEP THEM SIMPLE...

IF I TOUCH MY CAP LIKE THIS IT MEANS FOR WHOEVER HAPPENS TO BE ON BASE TO TRY TO STEAL...

IF I CLAP MY HANDS, IT MEANS THE BATTER IS TO HIT STRAIGHT AWAY, BUT IF I PUT THEM ON MY HIPS, THEN HE OR SHE IS TO BUNT...

IF I WALK UP AND DOWN IN THE COACHING BOX, IT MEANS FOR THE BATTER TO WAIT OUT THE PITCHER... IN OTHER WORDS, TO TRY FOR A WALK....

BUT NOW, AFTER ALL IS SAID AND DONE, IT MUST BE ADMITTED THAT SIGNALS ALONE NEVER WON A BALL GAME...

IT'S THE SPIRIT OF THE TEAM THAT COUNTS! THE **INTEREST** THAT THE PLAYERS SHOW IN THEIR TEAM! AM I RIGHT?

I SAID, AM I RIGHT?

3-27

Tm. Reg. U. S. Pat. Off.—All rights reserved
Copr. 1960 by United Feature Syndicate, Inc.

YOU'RE RIGHT... ＊SIGH＊

SCHULZ

55

PEANUTS
4-19
OH OH! HERE COMES "PIG-PEN"
SOMEDAY SOMEBODY'S GOING TO PUT FOUR BOARDS AROUND THAT KID AND HAVE AN "INSTANT SANDBOX"!
SCHULZ

PEANUTS
FORTY-EIGHT, FORTY-NINE, FIFTY! HERE I COME.. READY OR NOT!
4-20
RATS! I DON'T KNOW WHY I EVER PLAY THIS GAME!
SCHULZ

PEANUTS
ARE YOU INTERESTED IN PEDIATRICS, CHARLIE BROWN?
LISTEN TO THIS.."SOME NEWBORN INFANTS ARE HIGHLY INFECTIOUS TO OTHERS, AND BECAUSE THEY ARE LITERALLY SURROUNDED BY CLOUDS OF BACTERIA, THEY ARE CALLED 'CLOUD BABIES.'"
4-21
Tm. Reg. U. S. Pat Off.—All rights reserved Copr. 1960 by United Feature Syndicate, Inc.
WELL, WHAT ARE YOU LOOKING AT ME FOR?
SCHULZ

PEANUTS
by SCHULZ
GOOD GRIEF!
WHAT'S THE MATTER?
"WHAT'S THE MATTER?" HE ASKS!
"PIG-PEN," YOU'RE A DISGRACE!
NO GIRL COULD EVER LIKE ANYONE AS DIRTY AS YOU!
GIRLS LIKE BOYS WHO ARE CLEAN AND NEAT AND WHO KEEP THEIR SHOELACES TIED!
BUT THERE ARE A LOT OF THINGS MORE IMPORTANT THAN JUST BEING CLEAN!
Tm. Reg. U. S. Pat Off.—All rights reserved
Copr. 1961 by United Feature Syndicate, Inc.
SOMEHOW, I NEVER QUITE KNOW WHAT'S GOING ON...
2-12
SCHULZ

PEANUTS
"PIG-PEN," YOU'RE AN ABSOLUTE DISGRACE!
ALL THAT DIRT AND DUST... YOU COULD BE A **GERM CARRIER**...DID YOU EVER STOP TO THINK OF THAT?
SO WHAT IF I AM?
Tm. Reg. U. S. Pat. Off.—All rights reserved Copr. 1961 by United Feature Syndicate, Inc.
EVEN **GERMS** GET TIRED OF WALKING NOW AND THEN!
7-14
SCHULZ

PEANUTS
HOW WOULD YOU LIKE A GUM-DROP, CHARLIE BROWN?
I'VE ONLY HAD THEM IN MY POCKET FOR A WEEK..THERE'S SOME WHITE ONES, SOME PINK ONES, SOME RED ONES AND SOME BLACK ONES...
9/14
THEY **ALL** LOOK BLACK TO ME!
Tm. Reg. U. S. Pat. Off.—All rights reserved Copr. 1961 by United Feature Syndicate, Inc.
THEY DO TO ME, TOO...THAT'S VERY STRANGE
AND A LITTLE BIT NAUSEATING!
SCHULZ

PEANUTS
COUGH, PLEASE!
COUGH! COUGH! COUGH!
Tm. Reg. U. S. Pat. Off.—All rights reserved Copr. 1961 by United Feature Syndicate, Inc.
10-12
THESE COLD GERMS WILL NEVER BOTHER YOU AGAIN!
THANK YOU
STOMP STOMP STOMP
DO YOU THINK IT'S GOOD FOR YOUR PATIENTS TO BE LYING ON THE SIDEWALK THAT WAY?
NO WORSE THAN SITTING IN A DOCTOR'S COLD EXAMINING ROOM FOR FORTY MINUTES WHILE HE'S TREATING SOMEONE ELSE!
TRUE!
SCHULZ

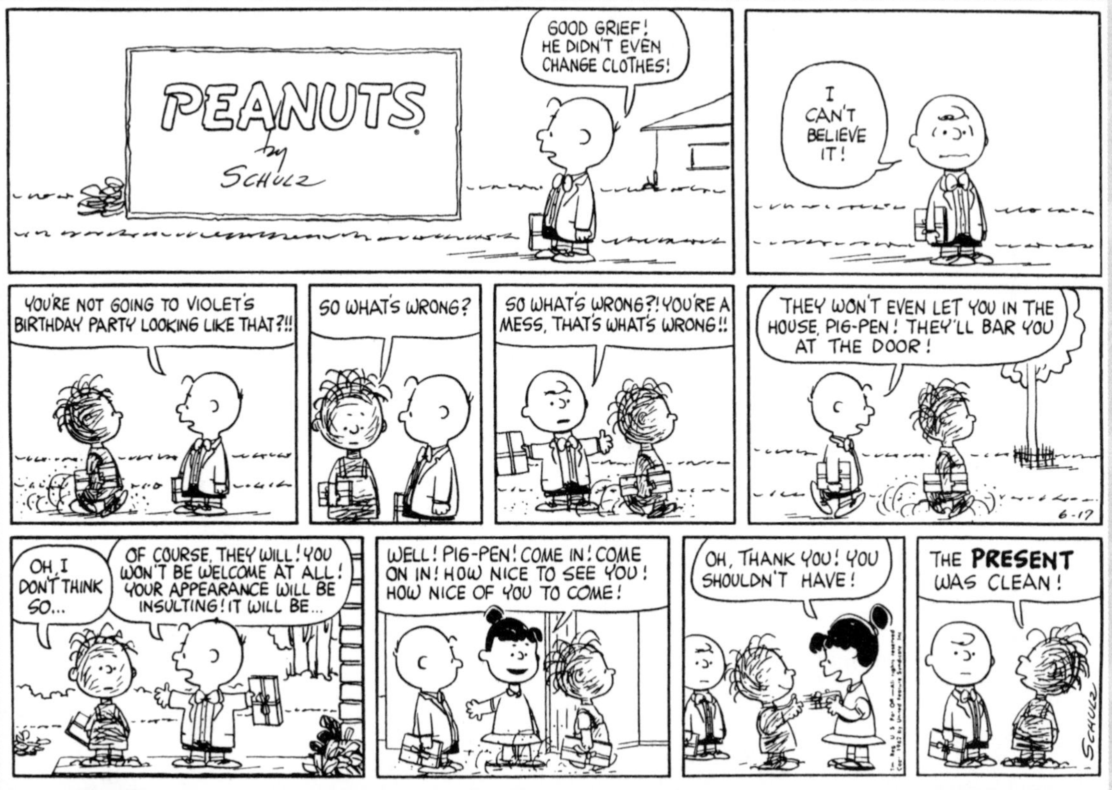
PEANUTS
by SCHULZ
GOOD GRIEF! HE DIDN'T EVEN CHANGE CLOTHES!
I CAN'T BELIEVE IT!
YOU'RE NOT GOING TO VIOLET'S BIRTHDAY PARTY LOOKING LIKE THAT?!!
SO WHAT'S WRONG?
SO WHAT'S WRONG?! YOU'RE A MESS, THAT'S WHAT'S WRONG!!
THEY WON'T EVEN LET YOU IN THE HOUSE, PIG-PEN! THEY'LL BAR YOU AT THE DOOR!
6-17
OH, I DON'T THINK SO...
OF COURSE, THEY WILL! YOU WON'T BE WELCOME AT ALL! YOUR APPEARANCE WILL BE INSULTING! IT WILL BE...
WELL! PIG-PEN! COME IN! COME ON IN! HOW NICE TO SEE YOU! HOW NICE OF YOU TO COME!
OH, THANK YOU! YOU SHOULDN'T HAVE!
THE **PRESENT** WAS CLEAN!
SCHULZ

PEANUTS 5-17

"PIG-PEN," YOU'RE A DISGRACE!

HERE IT IS, SPRINGTIME, AND THE WORLD IS BRIGHT, AND FRESH AND NEW...

AND HERE YOU ARE WITH THE SAME DIRTY OLD FACE!

I LOOK UPON MYSELF AS A CONNECTING-LINK WITH THE PAST

PEANUTS 4-7

Tm. Reg. U. S. Pat Off.—All rights reserved ©ar. 1966 by United Feature Syndicate, Inc.

I DON'T **WANT** ANOTHER RABIES SHOT!

PEANUTS

WHAT IN THE WORLD IS **THAT**?

THIS IS MY SPELLING PAPER..

YOU CAN'T TURN IN A SPELLING PAPER THAT LOOKS LIKE THAT, "PIG-PEN"! THERE'S DIRT ALL OVER IT! THAT'S THE MESSIEST-LOOKING PAPER I'VE EVER SEEN!

3-10

"PIG-PEN", YOU'LL GET A FAILING GRADE FOR SURE!

MAYBE YOU'RE RIGHT...

DO YOU HAVE A DIRT ERASER?

PEANUTS

PIG-PEN, YOU ARE A PERPETUAL MESS...

I CAN TELL JUST WHERE YOU'VE BEEN ALL WEEK FROM THE DIRT ON YOUR CLOTHES...YESTERDAY YOU WERE DOWN BY THE TRAIN TRACKS..

YOU SPENT THE DAY BEFORE DOWN AT THE PLAYGROUND, THE DUMP AND THE WAREHOUSE..

I DON'T HAVE TO LISTEN TO THIS..

AND MONDAY YOU SPENT ALL DAY AT THE BRICK YARD, ISN'T THAT RIGHT?

SCHULZ

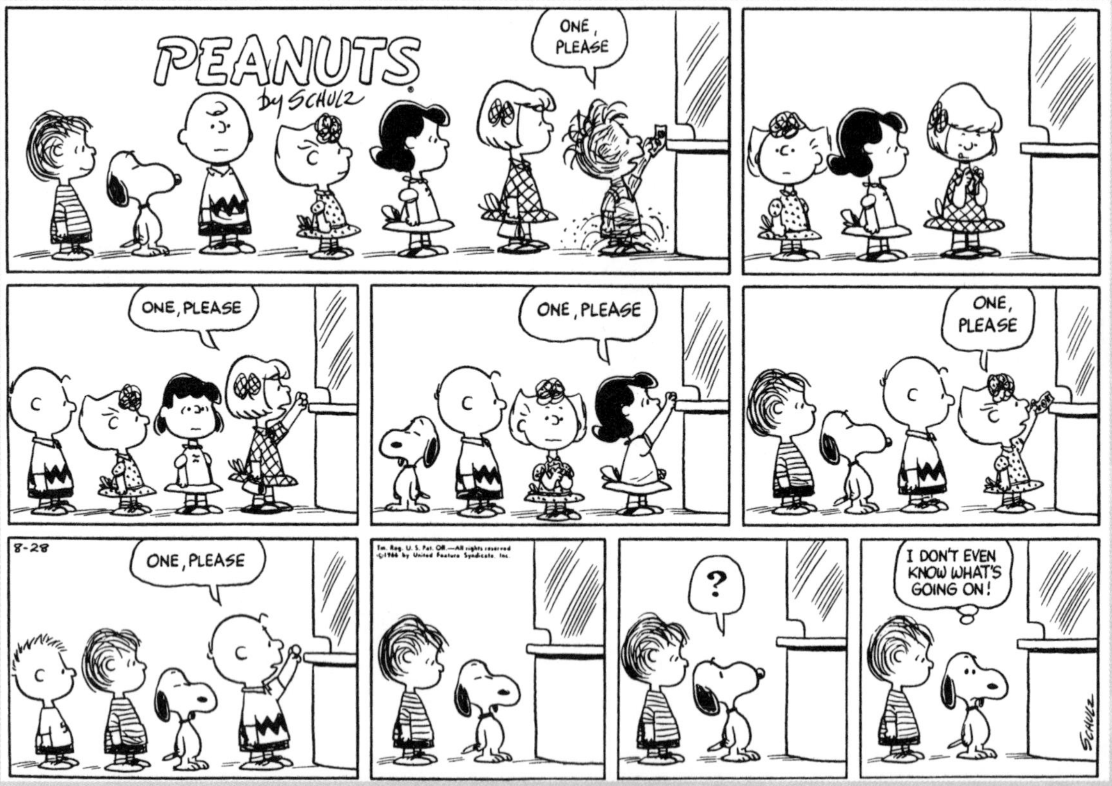
PEANUTS
by SCHULZ
ONE, PLEASE
ONE, PLEASE
ONE, PLEASE
ONE, PLEASE
8-28
ONE, PLEASE
Tm. Reg. U. S. Pat. Off.—All rights reserved
©1966 by United Feature Syndicate, Inc.
?
I DON'T EVEN KNOW WHAT'S GOING ON!
SCHULZ

PEANUTS
Tm. Reg. U. S. Pat. Off.—All rights reserved ©1967 by United Feature Syndicate, Inc.
HEY, C'MON! IT'S THE "ARM WRESTLING" CHAMPIONSHIP!
2-13
IT'S LUCY AGAINST THE "MASKED MARVEL"!
THEY'VE BEEN GOING AT IT FOR TWO HOURS NOW!
GIVE UP, YOU STUBBORN FEMALE!
CRACK, YOU STUPID BEAGLE!
SCHULZ

PEANUTS
Tm. Reg. U. S. Pat. Off.—All rights reserved ©1967 by United Feature Syndicate, Inc.
HAVE YOU EVER CONSIDERED WHAT A GOOD HUSBAND PIG-PEN WOULD MAKE?
8-15
UGH! I CAN'T IMAGINE ANYTHING WORSE!
ON THE CONTRARY...I THINK I'D BE A REAL BARGAIN...
SHE'D GET A HUSBAND AND AN ACRE OF GOOD TOPSOIL!
SCHULZ

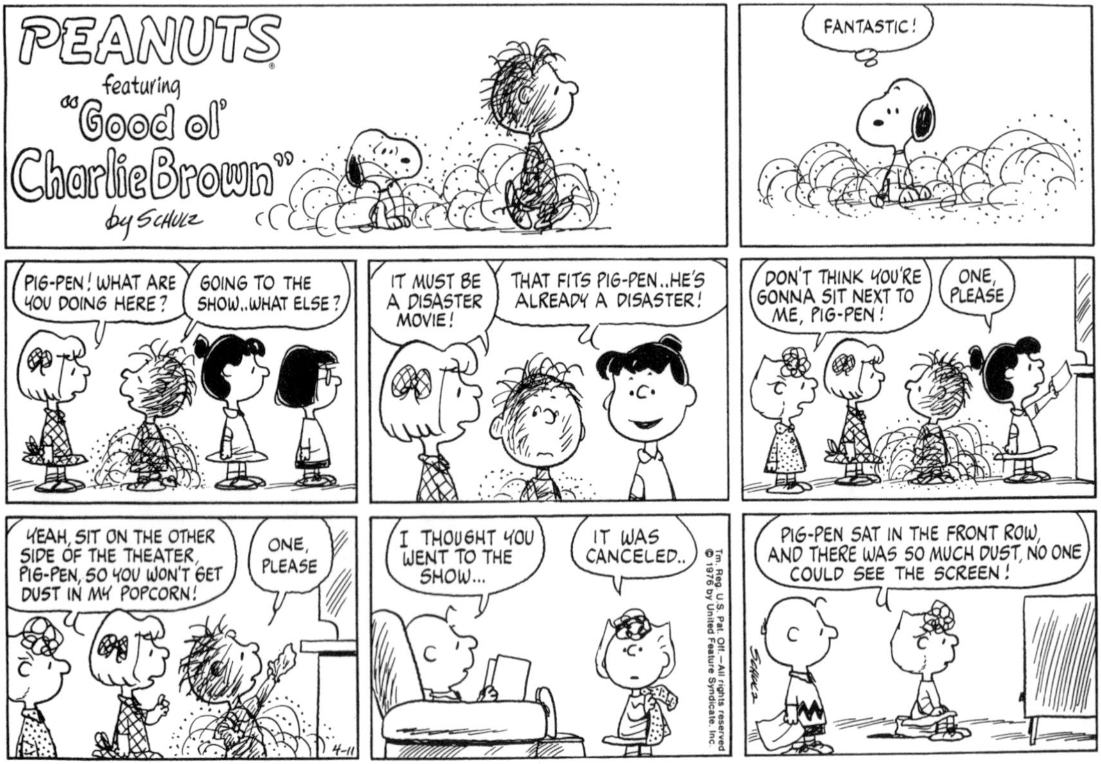
PEANUTS
featuring
"Good ol' Charlie Brown"
by SCHULZ
FANTASTIC!
PIG-PEN! WHAT ARE YOU DOING HERE?
GOING TO THE SHOW..WHAT ELSE?
IT MUST BE A DISASTER MOVIE!
THAT FITS PIG-PEN..HE'S ALREADY A DISASTER!
DON'T THINK YOU'RE GONNA SIT NEXT TO ME, PIG-PEN!
ONE, PLEASE
YEAH, SIT ON THE OTHER SIDE OF THE THEATER, PIG-PEN, SO YOU WON'T GET DUST IN MY POPCORN!
ONE, PLEASE
4-11
I THOUGHT YOU WENT TO THE SHOW...
IT WAS CANCELED..
Tm. Reg. U.S. Pat. Off.—All rights reserved © 1976 by United Feature Syndicate, Inc.
PIG-PEN SAT IN THE FRONT ROW, AND THERE WAS SO MUCH DUST, NO ONE COULD SEE THE SCREEN!
SCHULZ

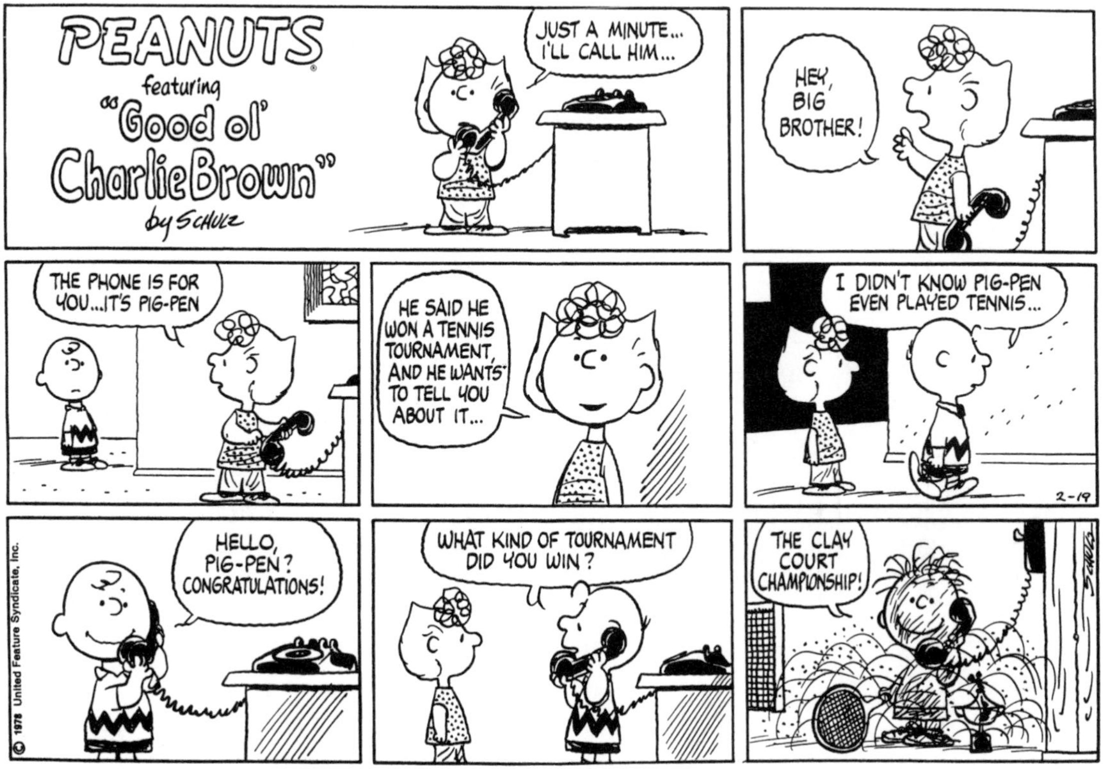
PEANUTS
featuring "Good ol' Charlie Brown"
by SCHULZ
JUST A MINUTE... I'LL CALL HIM...
HEY, BIG BROTHER!
THE PHONE IS FOR YOU...IT'S PIG-PEN
HE SAID HE WON A TENNIS TOURNAMENT, AND HE WANTS TO TELL YOU ABOUT IT...
I DIDN'T KNOW PIG-PEN EVEN PLAYED TENNIS...
2-19
© 1978 United Feature Syndicate, Inc.
HELLO, PIG-PEN? CONGRATULATIONS!
WHAT KIND OF TOURNAMENT DID YOU WIN?
THE CLAY COURT CHAMPIONSHIP!
SCHULZ

I THINK I'LL SIT HERE ON THE FRONT STEPS AND WAIT FOR MY DATE
© 1980 United Feature Syndicate, Inc.
A BOY LIKES TO KNOW A GIRL IS INTERESTED ENOUGH TO BE READY WHEN HE CALLS...
I WONDER WHO IT'S GOING TO BE..I HOPE HE'S A GOOD DANCER... IT'LL ALSO HELP IF HE'S A REAL SHARP DRESSER...
2-13
HI, MY NAME IS PIG-PEN
AAUGH!
SCHULZ

THIS IS SOME WEIRD DATE THAT CHUCK GOT FOR ME...
I MUST ADMIT HE CAN DANCE, THOUGH
2-14
WHAT'S YOUR SIGN, PIG-PEN? DO YOU COME HERE OFTEN?
WHERE DID HE GO?
© 1980 United Feature Syndicate, Inc.
SCHULZ

THAT WAS THE BEST VALENTINE'S DAY EVER, PIG-PEN!

I HAVEN'T HAD SO MUCH FUN AT A DANCE IN ALL MY LIFE!

2-15

♡ SMAK! ♡

© 1980 United Feature Syndicate, Inc.

WOW!

SCHULZ

I HEAR YOU HAD A GOOD TIME AT THE VALENTINE'S DAY DANCE, PIG-PEN...

YES, PATRICIA IS AN UNUSUAL GIRL.. DO YOU KNOW SHE NEVER ONCE CRITICIZED MY APPEARANCE?

2-18

I KNOW I'M NOT VERY NEAT, BUT I CAN'T SEEM TO CHANGE..

SCHULZ

© 1980 United Feature Syndicate, Inc.

NOT WITHOUT AN ENVIRONMENTAL IMPACT REPORT!

I'M TRYING TO WRITE PIG-PEN A NOTE, BUT I DON'T KNOW WHAT TO SAY

DON'T DO IT, SIR! DON'T LET HIM KNOW YOU LIKE HIM! FORCE HIM TO MAKE THE FIRST MOVE!

HOW DID YOU GET TO BE SUCH AN EXPERT, MARCIE?

© 1980 United Feature Syndicate, Inc.

2-19

ALL THE BEST COACHES ARE IN THE STANDS, SIR!

SCHULZ

 SEE, MARCIE? NO WORD FROM PIG-PEN! IF HE REALLY LIKED ME, HE WOULD HAVE CALLED OR WRITTEN BY NOW...

IT'S CHUCK'S FAULT! HE NEVER SHOULD HAVE ARRANGED FOR US TO GET TOGETHER!

2-20

I DON'T THINK YOU CAN REALLY BLAME CHUCK, SIR

© 1980 United Feature Syndicate, Inc.

YOU CAN IF YOU'RE UNREASONABLE!

SCHULZ

AS THE ANCIENT SAYING GOES, SIR, I HAVE SOME GOOD NEWS FOR YOU AND SOME BAD NEWS...
I TOOK IT UPON MYSELF TO CALL PIG-PEN.. HE ADMITTED THAT HE LIKED YOU...
2-21
© 1980 United Feature Syndicate, Inc.
HE ALSO SAID HE'S BEEN THINKING ABOUT ASKING YOU TO ANOTHER DANCE...
REALLY?
..NEXT VALENTINE'S DAY!
AAUGH!
SCHULZ

YOU AND PEPPERMINT PATTY HAVE BEEN SEEING A LOT OF EACH OTHER, HAVEN'T YOU?

YES, I THINK WHAT I LIKE ABOUT HER IS THAT SHE HASN'T TRIED TO CHANGE ME

© 1980 United Feature Syndicate, Inc.　3-3

I WONDER IF I COULD CHANGE HIM...

MARCIE, I CAME OVER BECAUSE I HAD TO TELL YOU THE CUTE THING PIG-PEN SAID TO ME

I'M NOT INTERESTED IN YOUR ROMANCE, SIR, AND I'M VERY BUSY PRACTICING THE ORGAN

© 1980 United Feature Syndicate, Inc.

MAY ALL YOUR HEMIDEMISEMIQUAVERS BE FLAT!!!

71

HEY, LUCILLE, YOU WANNA HEAR THE CUTE THING THAT PIG-PEN SAID TO ME YESTERDAY?
THIS WAS CUTE..THIS WAS REALLY CUTE...
3-5
HE......
© 1980 United Feature Syndicate, Inc.
RATS!
SCHULZ

HEY, SNOOP! LISTEN TO THE CUTE THING PIG-PEN SAID TO ME...
WE WERE WALKING ALONG, SEE, AND..
3-6
SUPPERTIME!
© 1960 United Feature Syndicate, Inc.
SCHULZ

PEANUTS featuring "Good ol' Charlie Brown" by SCHULZ
© 1960 United Feature Syndicate, Inc.
US MAIL
4-27
SCHULZ

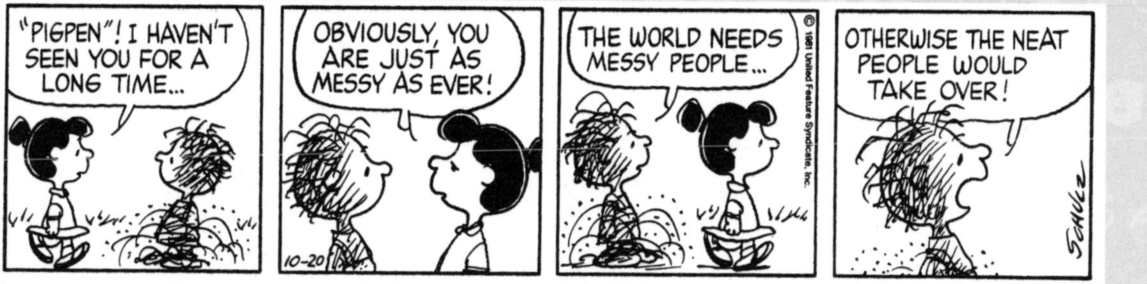
"PIGPEN"! I HAVEN'T SEEN YOU FOR A LONG TIME...
OBVIOUSLY, YOU ARE JUST AS MESSY AS EVER!
10-20
© 1981 United Feature Syndicate, Inc.
THE WORLD NEEDS MESSY PEOPLE...
OTHERWISE THE NEAT PEOPLE WOULD TAKE OVER!
SCHULZ

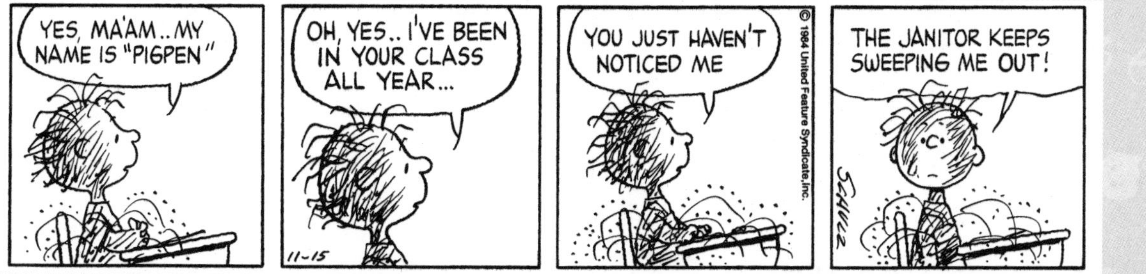
YES, MA'AM.. MY NAME IS "PIGPEN"
OH, YES.. I'VE BEEN IN YOUR CLASS ALL YEAR...
11-15
© 1984 United Feature Syndicate, Inc.
YOU JUST HAVEN'T NOTICED ME
THE JANITOR KEEPS SWEEPING ME OUT!
SCHULZ

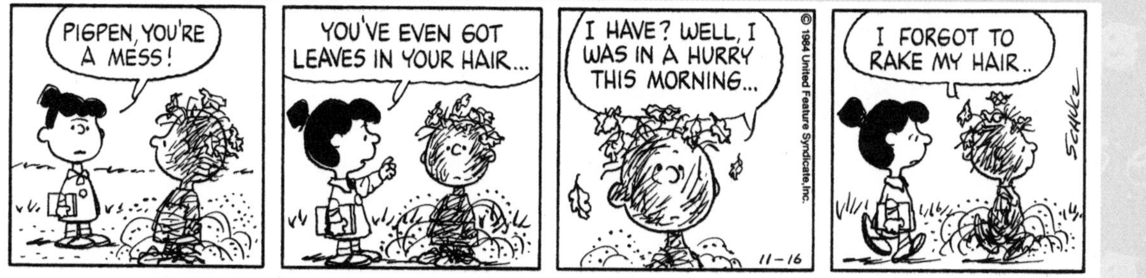
PIGPEN, YOU'RE A MESS!
YOU'VE EVEN GOT LEAVES IN YOUR HAIR...
© 1984 United Feature Syndicate, Inc.
I HAVE? WELL, I WAS IN A HURRY THIS MORNING...
11-16
I FORGOT TO RAKE MY HAIR..
SCHULZ

PEANUTS
featuring "Good ol' Charlie Brown"
by SCHULZ
I CAN HEAR HIM SNORING WAY OUT HERE..
TELL THE MANAGER
YEAH, IT'S HIS STUPID DOG!
Z
YOUR SHORTSTOP IS SOUND ASLEEP..
DON'T WORRY ABOUT IT...
7-14
© 1985 United Feature Syndicate, Inc.
SUPPERTIME!!
PLUNK!
AS THE YEARS GO BY, A GOOD MANAGER GETS TO KNOW HIS PLAYERS..
SCHULZ

PIGPEN, EVERY LITTLE MOVE YOU MAKE RAISES A CLOUD OF DUST!
I'M SORRY.. I CAN'T HELP IT
© 1985 United Feature Syndicate, Inc.
10-1
STOP BLINKING YOUR EYES!
SCHULZ

PSYCHIATRIC
HELP 5¢
I MEAN, HOW WOULD YOU LIKE TO GO THROUGH LIFE BEING CALLED 'PIGPEN'?
THE DOCTOR IS IN
3-8
HOW ABOUT YOUR FATHER? WHAT DO PEOPLE CALL HIM?
THE DOCTOR
© 1989 United Feature Syndicate, Inc.
'PIGPEN, SENIOR'!
THE DOCTOR IS IN
SCHULZ

PSYCHIATRIC
HELP 5¢

THE DOCTOR
IS IN

HERE'S SORT OF A SUGGESTION, "PIGPEN"..

© 1989 United Feature Syndicate, Inc.

MAYBE YOU COULD START BY TRYING TO GO FOR JUST ONE HOUR WITHOUT GETTING DIRTY.. WHAT WOULD HAPPEN IF YOU TRIED THAT?

DO YOU HAVE ANY IDEA HOW PAINFUL A MIGRAINE CAN BE?

3-9

THE DOCTOR IS IN

PSYCHIATRIC HELP 5¢
DO YOU THINK YOU'RE GOING TO BE ABLE TO HELP ME?
THE DOCTOR IS IN
I DON'T KNOW, "PIGPEN." WHEN I LOOK AT YOU, ALL I SEE IS DIRT AND DUST..YOU DON'T NEED A PSYCHIATRIST...
© 1989 United Feature Syndicate, Inc.
3-10
YOU NEED AN ARCHAEOLOGIST!
SCHULZ
THE DOCTOR IS IN

PEANUTS
by SCHULZ
EVERYBODY OUT FOR SPRING TRAINING!
WHAT HAPPENED TO WINTER?
3-12
BONK!
BONK!
WHIFF!
BONK!
© 1989 United Feature Syndicate, Inc.
WELL, HOW DOES THE OL' TEAM LOOK THIS YEAR, MANAGER?
IT'S HARD TO SAY, BUT I TRY TO BE OPTIMISTIC...
OPTIMISM IS ADMIRABLE IN A MANAGER, ISN'T IT? WHAT OTHER TRAITS DO YOU THINK YOU HAVE?
STUPIDITY!
SCHULZ

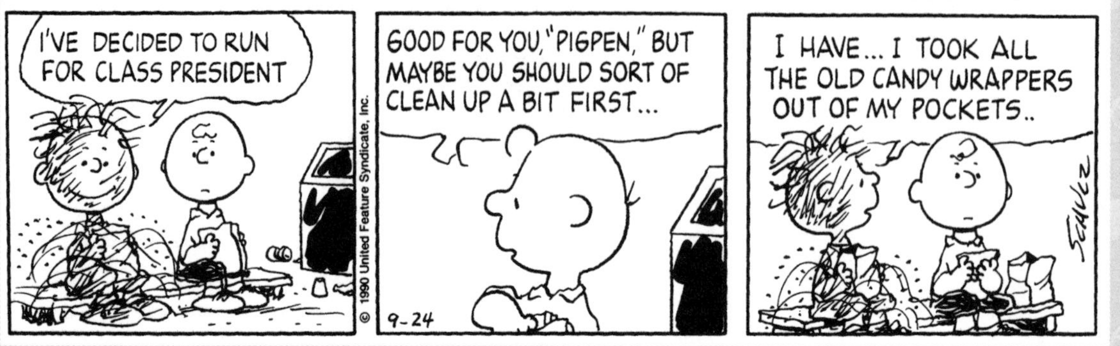
I'VE DECIDED TO RUN FOR CLASS PRESIDENT
GOOD FOR YOU, "PIGPEN," BUT MAYBE YOU SHOULD SORT OF CLEAN UP A BIT FIRST...
I HAVE... I TOOK ALL THE OLD CANDY WRAPPERS OUT OF MY POCKETS..
© 1990 United Feature Syndicate, Inc.
9-24
SCHULZ

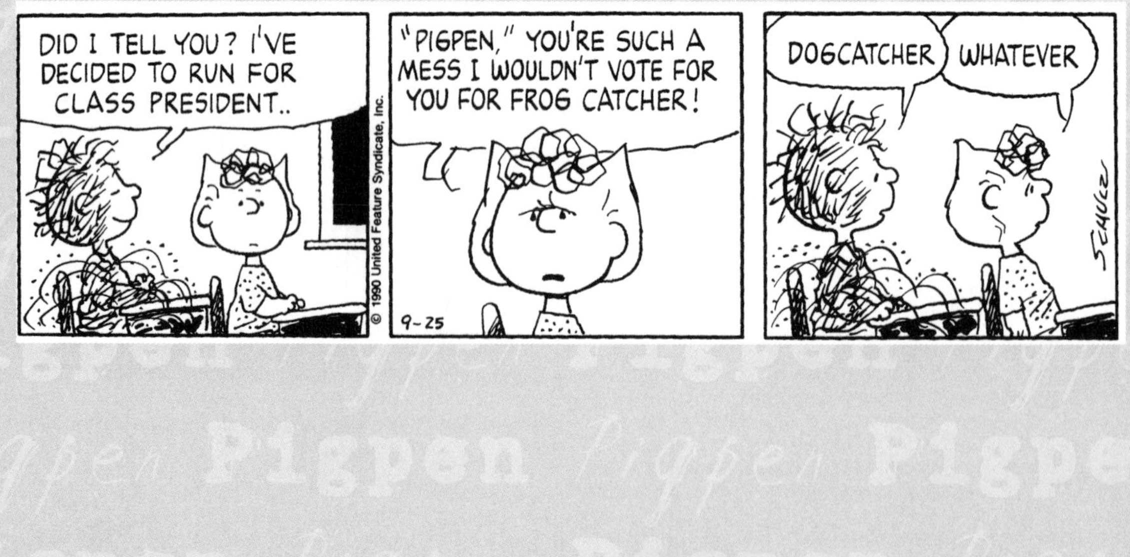
DID I TELL YOU? I'VE DECIDED TO RUN FOR CLASS PRESIDENT..
"PIGPEN," YOU'RE SUCH A MESS I WOULDN'T VOTE FOR YOU FOR FROG CATCHER!
DOGCATCHER
WHATEVER
© 1990 United Feature Syndicate, Inc.
9-25
SCHULZ

GUESS WHAT! I'VE DECIDED TO RUN FOR CLASS PRESIDENT! I'M GOING ON THE OL' CAMPAIGN TRAIL!
YOU LOOK MORE LIKE YOU JUST GOT OFF THE OLD CHISHOLM TRAIL!
SCHULZ
9-26
© 1990 United Feature Syndicate, Inc.

WHAT KIND OF A PHOTO DID YOU WANT, "PIGPEN"?
WELL, IF IT'S GOING TO BE A CAMPAIGN PHOTO, I FIGURED IT SHOULD HAVE A DOG IN IT...
© 1990 United Feature Syndicate, Inc.
OKAY, LET'S DO IT..
DON'T BOTHER MAKING ANY EXTRA PRINTS FOR ME..
SCHULZ
9-27

AND IF I'M ELECTED CLASS PRESIDENT, I PROMISE TO...
YOU CAN'T BE CLASS PRESIDENT, "PIGPEN"! YOU'RE A MESS, AND YOU HAVE NO DIGNITY!
© 1990 United Feature Syndicate, Inc.
9-28
SCHULZ

9-29
I'M SORRY YOU DIDN'T GET ELECTED CLASS PRESIDENT, "PIGPEN"
© 1990 United Feature Syndicate, Inc.
I THOUGHT HAVING A CAMPAIGN PHOTO OF ME AND A DOG WOULD DO IT...
NOBODY VOTED FOR ME..THEY ALL VOTED FOR THE DOG!

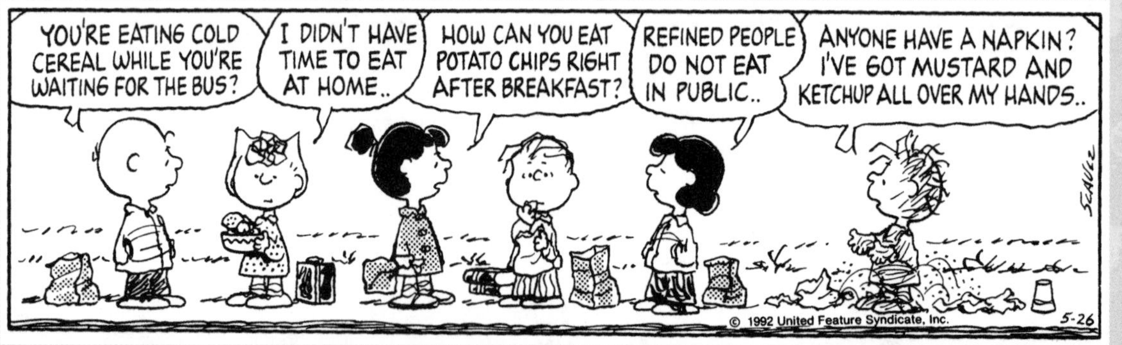
YOU'RE EATING COLD CEREAL WHILE YOU'RE WAITING FOR THE BUS?
I DIDN'T HAVE TIME TO EAT AT HOME..
HOW CAN YOU EAT POTATO CHIPS RIGHT AFTER BREAKFAST?
REFINED PEOPLE DO NOT EAT IN PUBLIC..
ANYONE HAVE A NAPKIN? I'VE GOT MUSTARD AND KETCHUP ALL OVER MY HANDS..
SCHULZ
© 1992 United Feature Syndicate, Inc.
5-26

"PIGPEN," THE TEACHER WANTS TO KNOW WHY THERE WAS MUSTARD AND KETCHUP ALL OVER YOUR HOMEWORK...
© 1992 United Feature Syndicate, Inc.
I WAS EATING A HOT DOG WHILE WE WERE WAITING FOR THE BUS, MA'AM...
MY DAD TOOK ME TO THE BALL GAME A FEW DAYS AGO, AND BOUGHT ME THREE HOT DOGS..
ONE OF THEM WAS STILL IN MY POCKET..
SCHULZ
5/27

HOW ARE THINGS IN LEFT FIELD, PIGPEN?
I PUT BURNT CORK UNDER MY EYES JUST LIKE THE PROS..
"PAINTING THE LILY," HUH?
PAINTING THE WHAT?
MANAGERS ARE ALWAYS SAYING STRANGE THINGS..
SCHULZ
3-19
© 1993 United Feature Syndicate, Inc.

ALL RIGHT, EVERYONE OVER HERE FOR THE TEAM PHOTO!
YOU HAVE YOUR CHOICE.. YOU CAN SIT WITH EITHER PIGPEN OR THE DOG...
WHAT KIND OF A CHOICE IS THAT?
I SHOULD THINK IT WOULD BE OBVIOUS
I'LL TAKE TEN 5X7, TWELVE 8X10, AND TWENTY WALLET SIZE..
SCHULZ
3-20
© 1993 United Feature Syndicate, Inc.

PEANUTS by SCHULZ

CAPS

WHAT'S GOING ON?

..AND EVERYONE WHO MADE THE TEAM THIS YEAR GETS A NEW CAP!

HERE YOU GO, SCHROEDER.. YOU DESERVE IT..

HERE YOU ARE, PIGPEN.. TRY TO KEEP IT CLEAN...

3-21

THIS IS FOR YOU, SNOOPY, OL' PAL!

HERE YOU GO, LINUS.. A BRAND NEW CAP!

© 1993 United Feature Syndicate, Inc.

I DON'T KNOW IF I MADE THE TEAM OR NOT..

SCHULZ

PEANUTS
by SCHULZ
OH, NO! LOOK WHO'S COMING..
THE DOCTOR IS IN
PSYCHIATRIC HELP 5¢
'PIGPEN,' YOU'RE A COMPLETE MESS!
THE DOCTOR IS IN
I WANT YOU TO GO HOME AND GET CLEANED UP..THEN WHEN YOU COME BACK, WE CAN HAVE A LITTLE TALK..
4-17
© 1994 United Feature Syndicate, Inc.
WOW! YOU LOOK GREAT! NOW WE CAN TALK ABOUT APPEARANCE, AND HOW IMPORTANT IT CAN BE...
THE DOCTOR
WE MAY NOT BELIEVE IT, BUT IT'S TRUE..
THE DOCTOR IS IN
WE MAY LIKE TO THINK APPEARANCE ISN'T..
THE DOCTOR IS IN
SIGH
THE DOCTOR IS IN

© 1994 United Feature Syndicate, Inc.

PEANUTS
by SCHULZ
A DIME?
FOR A DIME?
OKAY, I WROTE DOWN A NAME..NOW, YOU WRITE DOWN A NAME..DON'T LET ME SEE IT..
THIS IS FOR A DIME..
4-28
© 1996 United Feature Syndicate, Inc.
BONK!
I WIN! I WROTE DOWN "LUCY"!
SO DID I.. IT WAS A TIE!
SCHULZ

"PIGPEN," I DON'T UNDERSTAND YOU..
THIS IS THE FIRST INNING OF OUR FIRST GAME, AND YOU'RE ALREADY COVERED WITH DIRT..
THIS ISN'T ALL FROM TODAY.. SOME OF IT'S LEFT OVER FROM LAST YEAR..
www.unitedmedia.com
© 1997 United Feature Syndicate, Inc.
3-18
SCHULZ

DO ME A FAVOR..GO ASK "PIGPEN" WHY HE DOESN'T WEAR A BASEBALL CAP..
www.unitedmedia.com
THE MANAGER WANTS TO KNOW WHY YOU DON'T WEAR A CAP..
© 1997 United Feature Syndicate, Inc.
HE SAID HE DOESN'T WANT TO MUSS UP HIS HAIR..
SCHULZ
3-19

"PIGPEN," WHY CAN'T YOU LOOK NEAT LIKE THE OTHER PLAYERS?
www.unitedmedia.com
3-20
LAST YEAR I BATTED .712
© 1997 United Feature Syndicate, Inc.
NEATNESS DOESN'T BAT .712 !
SCHULZ

WAP!

3-21

"PIGPEN" SLIDES INTO HOME! HE'S SAFE! HE'S GETTING UP! HE'S DUSTING HIMSELF OFF..

WHY?

© 1997 United Feature Syndicate, Inc.

www.unitedmedia.com

YES, MA'AM.. "PIGPEN"

WELL, WHEN I LEFT HOME THIS MORNING, I WAS PRETTY CLEAN..

..SORT OF...RELATIVELY.. ..BORDERLINE...

ABSOLUTELY FILTHY..

© 1999 United Feature Syndicate, Inc.

www.snoopy.com

9-8